The Comedy Annual 2013

Compiled by Lynn Purdie
Designed by Sam Macnamara

A Pillar Box Red Publication

© 2012. Published by Pillar Box Red Publishing Ltd.

Images © Shutterstock.com

ISBN: 978-1-907823-42-8

£7.99

What's inside?

Another year, another annual full of jokes, puzzles and silliness for to keep you amused. Enjoy friends!
–Hardy Har

Contents

Fishy Fun!

What happened to the shark that swallowed a bunch of keys?
He got lockjaw!

What kind of fish goes well with ice cream?
Jellyfish!

What kind of money do fishermen make?
Net profits!

Why are goldfish orange?
The water makes them rusty!

What do you get from a bad-tempered shark?
As far away as possible!

Where do fish wash?
In a river basin!

What's the difference between a fish and a piano?
You can't tuna fish!

Where does seaweed look for a job?
In the 'Kelp-wanted' ads!

Where do little fishes go every morning?
To plaice school!

What fish goes up the river at 100mph?
A motor pike!

Which fish can perform operations?
A Sturgeon!

What did the boy fish say to his girlfriend?
'Your plaice or mine?'

Why is a fish easy to weigh?
Because it has its own scales!

What do you get if you cross an abbot with a trout?
Monkfish!

What kind of fish will help you hear better?
A herring aid!

Riddles & Rhymes

ZZZ...

How can a man go eight days without sleep?
-He sleeps at night.

How can you throw a ball as hard as you can and have it come back to you even if it doesn't hit anything, there is nothing attached to it and no one else catches or throws it?

-Throw the ball straight up in the air.

A cat had three kittens, January, March and May. What was the mother's name?

-What.

mine mine mine

What belongs to you, but others use it more than you do?

-Your name.

What is in seasons, seconds, centuries and minutes but not in decades, years or days?

-The letter 'n'.

What day has day in it but isn't Sunday, Monday, Tuesday, Wednesday, Thursday, Friday, or Saturday?

-Today!

What begins with T, ends with T and has T in it?

-A teapot.

What is the capital of Greece?

-G.

The more of them you take, the more you leave behind. What are they?

-Footsteps.

A man crosses a bridge and he sees a boat full of people, however there isn't a single person on board.
How can this be?

-Everyone is married!

A man is going on a trip with a horse. He leaves on Friday. He stays 3 days and comes back on Friday.
How is this possible?

-The horse's name is Friday!

What question can't you answer with yes?
-Are you asleep?

Bath Time

A bath without bubbles? You must be having a laugh!
Who'd want to sit in a boring old bath?
Fill it right to the top and even then don't you stop
Over the side they'll go as they start to flow
Onto the floor and out the bathroom door
Running down the stairs, bubbles EVERYWHERE
Creeping slowly along the ground and into the lounge
Soaking dad's feet as he snores asleep, in his seat
Into the kitchen, scaring Murphy the cat
Moving towards the back door and covering the mat
Out Murphy's flap and into the garden it goes
Under the bench, smothering the garden hose
Oops and blast! It's reaching the grass
What do I do now? I've got to stop it somehow?
I jump up through my bubbles and as I reach for the taps
I realise I'm daydreaming, and I start to giggle and laugh
See, didn't I tell you that bubbles were fun?
Especially when you pretend to let the bath overrun.

Sock Secret

I know you know that I know you know
Said the man in the shoe shop to the assistant named Joe
What do I know you know that I know said Joe?
You know, down there, on my foot below
Sir, I'm a little confused as to what you think that I know
Said Joe to the man as his confusion started to grow
The man pulls off his sock and says 'there you go'
All this fuss... for an extra toe!

WHAT AM I?

ACROSS

2 I have legs but cannot walk, you use me to rest. I am a _____ (5)

3 I was born in an egg. I peel like an onion but I still remain whole. I am a _____ (5)

7 You can throw me away but I will keep on coming back. I am a _____ (9)

8 I can go all around the world but I stay in one place. I cannot see, speak or hear, yet I have a face. I am a _____ (5)

11 I live in the sky. I am bright at night but I am not a light. I am a ____ (4)

12 You will see me in the grass, yellow like the sun. Then I change to dainty white and blow away. I am a _____ (9)

14 You serve me but I am never eaten. I am a _____ ____ (6,4)

15 I have a mouth but I cannot eat. I am a _____ (5)

DOWN

1 I have no beginning or end, I show my colours after the rain when the sun comes out. I am a _____ (7)

4 I go up and down stairs without moving. I am a _____ (6)

5 I can be tall or small, thick or thin. I like to be lit but don't like the wind. I am a _____ (6)

6 I am round like an apple but flat. I have eyes but can't see. I am a _____ (6)

7 I am black when I'm clean and white when I'm dirty. I am a _____ (10)

9 If you look at my front you see someone but if you look at my back you don't. I am a _____ (6)

10 I come in different shapes and sizes but I fit altogether. I am a _____ (6)

13 I have hands and a face but I cannot see. I am a _____ (5)

Answers on page 60

Tongue Twisters

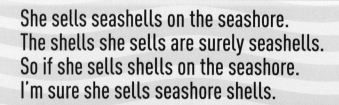

She sells seashells on the seashore.
The shells she sells are surely seashells.
So if she sells shells on the seashore.
I'm sure she sells seashore shells.

A tutor who tooted the flute.
Tried to tutor two tooters to toot.
Said the two to their tutor:
"Is it harder to toot,
Or to tutor two tooters the flute?"

A big black bear
bit a big black bug.
Then the big black bug
bled black blood.

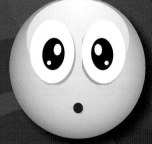

I've never smelled a smelt that smelled like that smelt smelled

Mr See owned a saw.
And Mr. Soar owned a seesaw.
Now, See's saw sawed Soar's seesaw
Before Soar saw See,
Which made Soar sore.
Had Soar seen See's saw
Before See sawed Soar's seesaw,
See's saw would not have sawed
Soar's seesaw.
So See's saw sawed Soar's seesaw.
But it was sad to see Soar so sore
just because See's saw sawed
Soar's seesaw.

The big black bug bit the big black bear,
but the big black bear bit the big black bug back!

One-one was a race horse.
Two-two was one too.
One-one won one race.
Two-two won one too.

If you notice this notice,
you will notice
that this notice
is not worth noticing.

Betty Bunter had some butter,
but her butter was a bit bitter.
If she baked with bitter butter,
it would make the batter bitter.
But a bit of better butter
that would make the batter better."
So she bought a bit of butter,
better than her bitter butter,
and she baked it in her batter,
and the batter was not bitter.
So 'twas better Betty Bunter
bought a bit of better butter.

Doctor, Doctor!

Doctor, Doctor, I think I'm a python.
You can't get round me just like that you know!

Doctor, Doctor, I swallowed a bone.
Are you choking?
No, I really did!

Doctor, Doctor, I think I'm suffering from Deja Vu!
Didn't I see you yesterday?

Doctor, Doctor, how do I stop my nose from running?
Stick your foot out and trip it up!

Doctor, Doctor, can I have a second opinion?
Of course, come back tomorrow!

Doctor, Doctor, I've broken my arm in two places.
Well don't go back there again then!

Doctor, Doctor, I think I'm a dog.
How long have you felt like this?
Ever since I was a puppy!

Doctor, Doctor, I think I'm turning into a frog?
Hop it!

Doctor, Doctor, I think I'm a yo-yo.
Are you stringing me along?

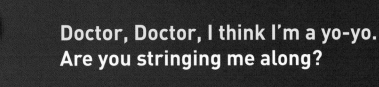

Doctor, Doctor, I feel like a needle.
I see your point!

Doctor, Doctor, I think I'm a bridge.
What's come over you?
Two cars, a large truck and a coach.

Doctor, Doctor, I think I'm an electric eel.
That's shocking!

Doctor, Doctor,, I feel like a pair of curtains.
Pull yourself together!

Doctor, Doctor, I feel like a race horse.
Take one of these every four laps.

15

Spot the

There are 6 differences between these two photographs. Can you spot them?

Differences

Answers on page 60

"Cross The Road" Corkers

Why did the chicken cross the road?
To get to the other side!

Why did the chicken cross the playground?
To get to the other slide!

What happened when the elephant crossed the road?
It stepped on the chicken!

Why did the duck cross the road?
To prove he wasn't chicken!

Why did the hedgehog cross the road?
Because he wanted to see his flat mate!

Why did the pig cross the road?
Because he didn't want to hog one side!

Why did the giraffe cross the road?
To visit the chicken!

Why did the monkey cross the road?
Because he was glued to the elephant that was taped to the
duck that was attached to the hedgehog that got a piggy back
ride on the pig that was stapled to the giraffe that was tied to the
chicken that crossed the road

Why did the banana cross the road?
Because it was running away from the monkey that was
glued to the elephant that was taped to the duck that was
attached to the hedgehog that got a piggy back ride on
the pig that was stapled to the giraffe that was tied to the
chicken that crossed the road

Why didn't the dinosaur cross the road?
Because roads weren't invented yet, silly!

Why did the one-handed man cross the road?
To get to the second hand shop

Why didn't the skeleton cross the road???
Because it had no guts!!

Why did the cow cross the road?
To get to the 'udder side'!

Why did the nose cross the road?
Because it kept getting picked on!!

There are two hedgehogs standing at the side of the road.
One turns to the other and says, "Shall we cross the road?"
The other one says, "No way!! Look what happened to the
zebra crossing!"

Why did the sheep cross the road?
To get to the 'baa baa' shop for a haircut.

Why did the dog cross the road?
To get to the 'barking' lot.

Why did the turtle cross the road?
To get to the Shell Station.

Why did the horse cross the road?
To reach his Neiiiiiiigh-borhood.

YOUR FAVOURITE

Skye, 6
What's black and white and makes a lot of noise?
A zebra with a drumkit.

Calvin, 9
What do you get from a pampered cow?
Spoiled milk.

Zakk, 7
Why do dragons sleep during the day?
So they can fight knights.

Josh, 7
How do you catch a squirrel?
Climb up a tree and act like a nut.

Ellie, 5
Where do fish keep their money?
In the river bank!

FUNNIES

Hannah, 5

What did the zebra say when it crossed the road?

Now you see me now you don't.

Kirsty, 8

Why did the sheep cross the road?

Because it wanted to get to the Baaaarbers.

Iona , 9
Knock Knock
Who's there?
Someone.
Someone who?
Someone who can't reach the doorbell.

Connor , 9

How do you make a tissue dance?

Put a little boogey in it!

Roan, 7

What did the water say to the boat?

Nothing, it just waved.

Chloe, 11

What did the judge say when the skunk walked into the court room?

Odour in the court.

Join the dots and
colour in the shapes
to see what you get?

22

Party Time!

Musical Madness

What is the most musical bone?
The Trombone!

What makes music on your head?
A head band!

Why was the musician arrested?
Because he got in treble!

Where did the music teacher leave her keys?
In the piano!

How do you make a bandstand?
Take away their chairs!

What's a rabbit's favourite music?
Hip Hop!

DID YOU

The strongest muscle in the body is the tongue.

A rhinoceros horn is made of compacted hair.

It is impossible to sneeze with your eyes open.

A snail can sleep for 3 years.

Our eyes are always the same size from birth, but our nose and ears never stop growing.

A polar bear's skin is black. Its fur is not white, but actually clear.

TYPEWRITER, is the longest word that can be made using the letters on only one row of the keyboard.

A crocodile cannot stick its tongue out.

The word racecar and kayak are the same whether they are read left to right or right to left.

Butterflies taste with their feet.

KNOW???

Rubber bands last longer when refrigerated.

Tigers have striped skin, not just striped fur.

The microwave was invented after a researcher walked by a radar tube and a chocolate bar melted in his pocket.

Elephants are the only animals that can't jump.

The average person falls asleep in seven minutes.

There are more chickens than people in the world.

A cat has 32 muscles in each ear.

There are 336 dimples on a regulation golf ball.

A shark is the only fish that can blink with both eyes.

"I am." is the shortest complete sentence in the English language.

Wacky Wordsearch

Can you find the words hidden in the grid? Words can go horizontally, vertically and diagonally in all directions.

Birthday	Hobby
Celebrate	Love
Clouds	Marshmallows
Comic	Merry
Cool	Pillows
Daisies	Silly
Delightful	Snuggles
Glee 	Strawberries
Happy	Yummy

Answers on page 60

V T D S J M J N R M K Y B B O H

R F B E Z N F Y R F N L X J C G

K H T I L R P M P J M W W R R Y

Z G K R G I Q L M P L V T G M H

T L D R H C G R F L A B N M Y S

R E P E N C M H O P I H U R T W

C E I B P I S O T R M Y L T Q O

G T L W Z M C D T F M E Y N D L

F F L A F O M H U X U E R L H L

Z Q O R R C D H Z O V L D R K A

Q R W T L A V Q S O L T X Y Y M

N X S S Y D N I L V D C J T D H

E T A R B E L E C V M W K M N S

L N M K T L D A I S I E S K K R

T V V G Y Z D T L F B J H Q R A

D W S N U G G L E S T N K L X M

Funny Food Frolics

-Why did the baker stop making doughnuts?
She was bored with the hole business!

-What do you get when you cross a snake and a pie?
A pie-thon!

-Why do toadstools grow so close together?
Because they don´t need mushroom.

-What is a scarecrow's favourite fruit?
Straw-berries!

-What day do potatoes hate the most?
Fry-day!

-Why did the kid throw the butter out the window?
To see the butter fly!

-What's the worst vegetable to serve on a boat?
Leeks!

-What did the nut say when it sneezed?
Cashew!

-How do you make an apple turnover?
Roll it down a hill

-Why are bananas never lonely?
Because they hang around in bunches

-How can you spell candy with two letters?
C and Y.

-What do you get if you cross a biscuit with a tuxedo?
A smart cookie.

-Why couldn't the teddy bear
eat his lunch?
Because he was stuffed!

-Why did the apple go out with a fig?
It couldn't find a date!

-What do polar bears eat for lunch?
Ice berg-ers!

-Why are sausages rude?
Because they spit at you while they are cooking.

-Why did the pickle stay in bed?
He felt dill.

-What do you call a rich melon?
Melon-aire.

-What´s yellow and swings from cake to cake?
Tarzipan.

-Why did the potato go out with the mushroom?
Because he was a fungi to be with.

Hink Pinks to Make you Think

Hello friends!
Have you heard of
a Hink Pink before?
Not to worry if you haven't,
I'm here to help you.

A Hink Pink is a pair of rhyming words that match a silly definition. Sometimes they are called 'Ryhming Pairs' too.
Let me show you an example and then see if you can guess mine below?

Example: **Definition - A black bird that doesn't fly very fast**

Rhyming words – Slow crow

Did you get it? I've given you a clue for each one by telling you what the first letter of each word is.

Good luck!

Rabbit that tells jokes: F_ _ _ _ B_ _ _ _ _

Chunky feline: F _ _ C _ _

Her Royal Highness's denim pants: Q _ _ _ _ ' _ J _ _ _ _

Non clever guy who shoots arrows on Valentine's Day: S _ _ _ _ _ _ C _ _ _ _ _

Pet pooch in the rain: S _ _ _ _ D _ _ _ _

A reptile magician: L _ _ _ _ _ _ W _ _ _ _ _ _

Lengthy Tune: L _ _ _ _ S _ _ _

Light red beverage: P _ _ _ D _ _ _ _ _

Unhappy father: S _ _ D _ _

Fast elevator: S _ _ _ _ _ L _ _ _ _

Stinging insect that doesn't cost money: F _ _ _ B _ _

A married rodent: M _ _ _ _ S _ _ _ _ _ _

Answers on Page 60

CRAZY CROSSWORD

I AM A...

ACROSS

4   I live in a house called a coop. I have two legs, two wings and a tail. I eat worms and bugs and grain. I lay eggs. I am a _____ (7)

5   I'm very, very big. I like to eat peanuts and hay. I have four legs and two big ears. My long nose is called a trunk. I am an __(8)___

7   I have four legs and a long tail. I eat oats and hay. I love to run fast. I let people ride on my back. I am a _____ (5)

8   I am small and shy. I have eight legs. I eat bugs. I catch them in my web. I am a _____ (6)

10   My skin is green and slippery. I have four legs and webbed feet. I eat bugs and little fish. I can swim under water and hop on land. I am a ____ (4)

DOWN

1   I live in the ocean. I like to eat crabs. I can change colours. My eight legs are called tentacles. I am an _____ (7)

2   I have wings but I'm not a bird. I am small and colourful. I live in gardens and fields and forests. I used to be a caterpillar. I am a _____ (9)

3   I live in the ocean. I move slowly. I eat clams. I have five arms. I am a _____ (7)

6   I have a tail. I can fly. I'm covered in colourful feathers. I can whistle and I can talk. I am a _____ (6)

9   I have four legs. I'm very smart and I like to play. I like to smell things. I can wag my tail. I am a ___ (3)

Answers on page 60

Laughing Cats & Dogs

Ha Ha!

Did you hear about the cat that swallowed a ball of wool?

She had mittens.

What goes "tick tock, woof woof"?

A watch dog.

What do cats like on a hot day?

A mice cream cone.

What do you get when you cross a dog and a phone?

A Golden Receiver.

What do cats like to eat for breakfast?

Mice Krispies.

What do you get if you cross a sheepdog with a rose?

A collie-flower!

What do you call a cat that lives in the desert?

Sandy Claws.

What has more lives than a cat?

A frog. It croaks every night.

What happened when the dog went to the flea circus?

He stole the show!

What kind of cats like to go bowling?
Alley cats.

What do you call a great dog detective?
Sherlock Bones.

Where do cats go when they lose their tales?
The Retail Store!

What is a cat's favourite song?
Three Blind Mice!

What does a dog get when it finishes obedience school?
A pet degree.

What is a cat's favourite colour?
Purrrrrrrple!

How do cats end a fight?
They hiss and make up!

Why was the dog sweating so much?
Because he was a hotdog.

Ha Ha!

The Numbers Game

 I'm now a 4 because I've lost 3. Can you guess what number I used to be?

 Hello friends, my name is 7. What number would you add to make me 11?

 Right now I'm 5 but what would I be, if you were to multiply me by 3?

 Add me to 1 and what will I become? Then divide me by 4 to find out the score.

 Before adding 13, what would I have been? Now to that number add some more, how about 4?

 Multiply me by 3 then subtract 2 and 1, now divide me by 3 and tell me what have I become?

 Some say I'm unlucky, I say I am great! What number would you subtract from me to turn me into 8?

 If you divided me by 2 and then added me to 10, subtracted my original number then another 3, what would I be then?

Answers on page 61

Tongue Twisters

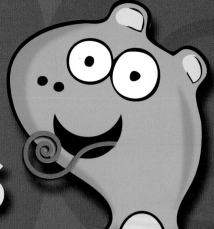

How much wood would a woodchuck chuck,
If a woodchuck could chuck wood?
A woodchuck would chuck all the wood he could chuck,
If a woodchuck could chuck wood.

Peter Piper picked a peck of pickled peppers.
A peck of pickled peppers Peter Piper picked.
If Peter Piper picked a peck of pickled peppers.
How many pickled peppers did Peter Piper pick?

Round and round the rugged rock the ragged rascal ran.

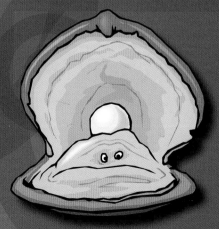

A noisy noise annoys an oyster!

A tree-toad loved a she-toad,
Who lived up in a tree.
He was a two-toed tree-toad,
But a three-toed toad was she.
The two-toed tree-toad tried to win
The three-toed she-toad's heart,
For the two-toed tree-toad loved the ground
That the three-toed tree-toad trod.
But the two-toed tree-toad tried in vain;
He couldn't please her whim.
From her tree-toad bower,
With her three-toed power,
The she-toad vetoed him.

Whether the weather be fine
or whether the weather be not.
Whether the weather be cold
or whether the weather be hot.
We'll weather the weather
whether we like it or not.

If two witches would
watch two watches,
which witch
would watch
which watch?

The sixth sick sheik's sixth sheep's sick

How many cookies could a good cook cook,
if a good cook could cook cookies?
A good cook could cook as many cookies as a good cook could,
as long as the good cook cooked cookies.

YOUR FAVOURITE

Hollie, 6
What did the elf use to make him taller?
Elf raising flour.

Leo, 7
Why did the pirate cross the road?
To get to the other tide.

Julia, 8
What's green and hairy and goes up and down?
A gooseberry in a lift.

Antonia, 8
Doctor, Doctor, I keep getting pain in my mouth.
Have you tried taking the spoon out?

Daniel, 8
Why did the snooker player go to the toilet?
To pot a brown.

FUNNIES

Ewan ,9
Doctor, Doctor, I feel like a pack of cards
I'll deal with you later.

Adam, 8
Did you hear the bin man's joke?
It was rubbish!

Charlie, 9
Why was the broom late?
It over swept!

Eirinn, 11
What do you call a cow with a twitch?
Beef jerky.

Emma, 5
What did the bee say to the flower?
Hi honey.

Jamie, 9
Why is it so hot in a stadium after a football game?
Because all the fans have left.

Spot the

There are 6 differences between these two photographs. Can you spot them?

Differences

Doctor, Doctor!

Doctor, Doctor, will this cream help clear my spots?
I never make rash decisions.

Doctor, Doctor, When I press with my finger here... it hurts, and here... it hurts, and here... and here... What do you think is wrong with me?
You have a broken finger!

Doctor, Doctor, I've just swallowed a roll of film.
Well let's just wait and see if anything develops!

Doctor, Doctor, I feel like an apple.
We must get to the core of this!

Doctor, Doctor, I keep seeing an insect spinning in circles.
Don't worry, it's just a bug that's going around!

Doctor, Doctor, I keep seeing double.
Take a seat on the couch.
Which one!

Doctor, Doctor, everyone thinks I'm a liar
Well I don't believe that!

Doctor, Doctor,, some days I feel like a tee-pee and other days I feel like a wig-wam.
You're too tents.

Doctor, Doctor, I keep seeing
spots before my eyes.
Have you seen a Doctor already?
No, just spots.

Doctor, Doctor,, I feel like a carrot.
Don't get yourself in a stew.

Doctor, Doctor,, I've swallowed my pocket money.
Take this and we'll see if there's any change in the morning.

Doctor, Doctor,, I've heard that exercise kills germs, is it true?
Probably, but how do you get the germs
to exercise?

Doctor, Doctor, I feel like a pony!
Don't worry, you're just a little hoarse.

Doctor, Doctor, every time I stand up quickly, I see Mickey
Mouse, Donald Duck and Goofy
How long have you been getting these Disney spells?

47

Fairy Tale Ticklers

Why wasn't Cinderella any good at soccer?
She kept running away from the ball!

Does the Little Mermaid use a knife and fork when she eats?
No, she uses her fish fingers!

Why did Rapunzel go to a lot of parties?
Because she liked to let her hair down!

What's brown, furry and has twelve paws?
The Three Bears!

How did Jack know how many beans his cow was worth?
He used a cowculator!

What kind of pet did Aladdin have?
A flying car-pet!

What did Snow White say to the photographer?
Someday my prints will come.

Where do mermaids go to see movies?
The dive-in.

What has green hair and runs from bears?
Mouldy locks

Which side of the Ugly Duckling has the most feathers?
The outside!

How did Jack know how many beans his cow was worth?
He used a cowculator!

What has six legs, four ears and a shining suit of armour?
A prince on horseback!

... and they all lived Hardily ever after

Wacky Wordsearch

Can you find the words hidden in the grid? Words can go horizontally, vertically and diagonally in all directions.

Balloons	Lollipops
Blissful	Lovely
Cute	Magical
Dance	Melody
Dimples	Pleasant
Grin	Rainbow
Hello	Shine
Holiday	Smile
Jelly	Yippee

Answers on page 61

```
B A L L O O N S X L S S Y
D M W L R R W Z P E H S Z
M B L I S S F U L I P L P
N E Y D P N R P N O Y J R
H G N D G Q M E P D E W T
Y R C A O I C I L L G O Y
A I H N D L L U L H H B L
D N H C G L E Y T M Y N E
I D Z E O C J M I E R I V
L N H L Z H M Q Y P F A O
O Y P E L I M S Y R P R L
H T W P L E A S A N T E R
M A G I C A L Q K H N H E
```

Easter
Eggs - Travaganza

What do you call a bunny with fleas?
Bugs Bunny!

Why was the Easter Bunny so upset?
He was having a bad hare day!

What did one coloured egg say to the other?
Heard any good yolks lately?

How does the Easter bunny stay in shape?
Lots of eggs-ercise!

What do you call a line of rabbits walking backwards?
A receding hareline.

How do you know carrots are good for your eyes?
Have you ever seen a rabbit with glasses?

How can you tell which rabbits are the oldest in a group?
Just look for the grey hares.

What do you get when you cross a bunny with an onion?
A bunion.

How does an Easter chicken bake a cake?
From scratch.

How many chocolate bunnies can you put into an empty Easter basket?
Only one because after that, it's not empty!

How did the soggy Easter Bunny dry himself?
With a hare dryer!

Where do Easter bunnies dance?
At the basket ball.

Ha Ha Halloween

Why can't ghosts play music in church?
Because they have no organs!

What is a vampire's favourite holiday?
Fangs-giving!

Why would mummies make good secret agents?
Because they keep things under wraps!

What do you get when you put a snowman in a haunted house?
Ice screams!

Why are graveyards noisy?
Because of the coffin!

How do you unlock a haunted house?
With a skeleton key!

What is the problem with twin witches?
You can never tell which witch is which!

What do sea monsters eat for lunch?
Fish and ships!

What do you call a ghost that puts out fires?
A fire frighter!

Why did Dracula fail art class?
Because he could only draw blood!

What did the skeleton buy at the market?
Spare ribs!

What is a ghost's favourite position in soccer?
Ghoul keeper!

COUNT DRACUHAR WISHES YOU A SPOOKY HALLOWEEN!

Christmas Cackles

Why does Santa Claus like to go down the chimney?
Because it soots him!

What do you call a snowman in the summer?
A puddle!

How much did Santa pay for his sleigh?
Nothing, it was on the house!

How does a snowman get to work?
By icicle

What do Snowmen call their offspring?
Chill-dren.

What is green, covered with tinsel and goes ribbet ribbet?
Mistle-toad!

What do you get if you cross an apple with a Christmas tree?
A pineapple!

Who is never hungry at Christmas?
The turkey - he's always stuffed!

What did one Angel say to the other?
Halo there!

What is white and red and blue at Christmas time?
A sad candy cane!

How do you scare a snowman?
You get a hairdryer!

What goes Ho, Ho, Swoosh! Ho, Ho, Swoosh?
Santa caught in a revolving door!

57

Bake me a Cake
.......with Megan x

"I love rainbow cupcakes because they are colourful and fun to make!"

Rainbow Cupcakes
Makes: 16
Total time: 25 mins
Skill level: Easy peasy

Cupcake Ingredients:

White Cake Mix – 525g
(alternatively you can make your own)
Food Colouring – Red, Yellow, Green and Blue
(mix colours to make purple and orange)

Topping Ingredients:

White Chocolate – 100g
Unsalted Butter – 140g
Icing Sugar – 250g

What else you will need:

An adult (to be your assistant and look after the oven. Hot, hot, hot!)
Cupcake tray
Cupcake Cases
Piping Bag and Nozzle
Food Colouring Measures:
Purple = 9 red and 6 blue drops
Blue = 12 drops blue
Green = 12 drops green
Yellow = 12 drops yellow
Orange = 12 yellow and 4 red drops
Red = 18 drops red

Prepare the white cake mix to the instructions given, and then divide the mix evenly among six small bowls. Dye each bowl of cake mix a rainbow colour with the specified amounts of food colouring drops.

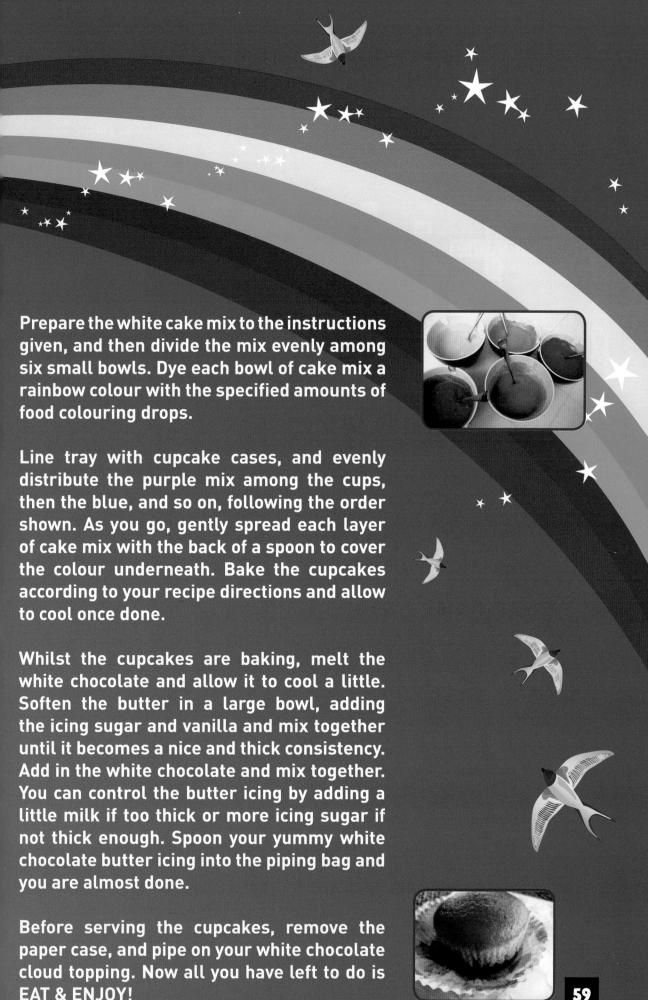

Line tray with cupcake cases, and evenly distribute the purple mix among the cups, then the blue, and so on, following the order shown. As you go, gently spread each layer of cake mix with the back of a spoon to cover the colour underneath. Bake the cupcakes according to your recipe directions and allow to cool once done.

Whilst the cupcakes are baking, melt the white chocolate and allow it to cool a little. Soften the butter in a large bowl, adding the icing sugar and vanilla and mix together until it becomes a nice and thick consistency. Add in the white chocolate and mix together. You can control the butter icing by adding a little milk if too thick or more icing sugar if not thick enough. Spoon your yummy white chocolate butter icing into the piping bag and you are almost done.

Before serving the cupcakes, remove the paper case, and pipe on your white chocolate cloud topping. Now all you have left to do is EAT & ENJOY!

Quiz Answers

What Am I crossword, page 10

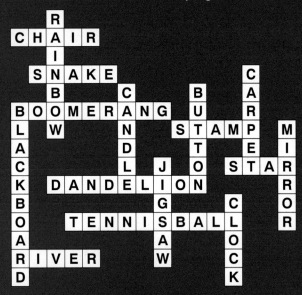

Spot the differences, page 16

Hink Pinks, page 33

Funny Bunny

Fat Cat

Queen's Jeans

Stupid Cupid

Soggy Doggy

Lizard Wizard

Long Song

Pink Drink

Sad Dad

Swift Lift

Free Bee

Mouse Spouse

Wacky Wordsearch, page 28

I Am A crossword, page 34

The Numbers Game, page 38

4 – I'm now a 4 because I've lost 3. Can you guess what number I used to be?

4 + 3 = 7 Answer – 7

7 – Hello friends, my name is 7. What number would you add to make me 11?

7 + 4 = 11 Answer – 4

5 – Right now I'm 5 but what would I be, if you were to multiply me by 3?

3 x 5 = 15 Answer – 15

9 – Add me to 1 and what will I become? Then divide me by 4 to find out the score.

9 + 1 = 10 ÷ 4 = 2½ Answer – 2½

15 – Before adding 13, what would I have been? Now to that number add some more, how about 4?

15 – 13 = 2 + 4 = 6 Answer – 6

2 – Multiply me by 3 then subtract 2 and 1, now divide me by 3 and tell me what I have become?

2 x 3 = 6 – 2 = 4 – 1 = 3 ÷ 3 = 1 Answer – 1

13 – Some say I'm unlucky, I say I am great! What number would you subtract from me to turn me into 8?

13 – 5 = 8 Answer – 5

6 – If you divided me by 2 and then added me to 10, subtracted my original number plus another 3, what would I be then?

6 ÷ 2 = 3 + 10 = 13 – 6 = 7 – 3 = 4 Answer - 4

Spot the differences, page 44

Wacky Wordsearch, page 50

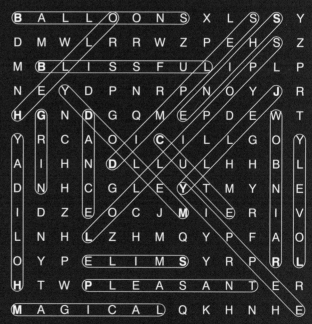

Where's
Hardy Har?